THE GOSPEL OF APOLLONIUS OF TYANA

(1900)

HIS LIFE AND DEEDS

ACCORDING TO PHILOSTRATOS

Kenneth S. Guthrie

ISBN 1-56459-943-4

Kenneth Sylvan Launfal Guthrie

(Harvard and Sewanee) ; Ph. D. (Columbia and Tulane) ; M. D. (Pennsylvania).
Professor in Extension, University of the South, Sewanee.
Address: Teocalli, 1177 Warburton Avenue, North Yonkers, N. Y.

ous of keeping informed of his latest achievements, send him one dollar
r a yearly subscription to his inspirational bi-monthly Magazine
GOOD NEWS FOR ALL.

TABLE OF CONTENTS

Life of Apollonius of Tyana.

BOOK FIRST

His Education.

Apollonius was born in Tyana, a Hellenic city of the Cappadocians, in Asia Minor. His family was noble, and, as wealth went in Tyana, of extraordinary wealth. Ther are legends of supernatural experiences said to have happened to his mother when she conceived and bore him.

Even during the years of his early education he showed much power of memory and strength of thought; he spoke pure Attic, and was noteworthy · for his beauty. When fourteen years of age his father took him to Tarsus in Cilicia, where he took instruction from the Phoenician Euthydemus. But he was not satisfied here, because the people were given up to luxury, and he retired with his teacher to the neighbouring city of Ægae, where was a temple of Æsculapius, and where he came in contact with teachers of various philosophical systems.

The man who taught him the Pythagorean doctrines, which he professed in after life, was no exalted moral example, his name was Euxenus, and 'he knew the doctrines of Pythagoras as much as birds (parrots) know the speech of man'. Nevertheless Apollonius studied under him for two years at the end of which time he forsook Euxenus; not unkindly indeed, but firmly. He besought his father for the gift of a small property just outside the city, full of gardens and rivulets, and presented it to his former teacher with these words: 'Live thou here according to thy manner of life—I propose to live according to the morals of Pythagoras.'

Staggered at this treatment, Euxenus asked him what he purposed to begin with? He answered, 'With' what the physicians begin—in that they cleanse the entrails; thus they preserve themselves better in health, and heal others.'

In accordance with this decision he avoided as unclean all animal food, limiting himself to fruit and vegetables. He avoided wine also, not because it came from so mild a plant as the vine, but because it confused the quiet order of reason, 'darkening the clear aether of the soul.' He wore linen garments, let his hair grow, and dwelt in the the temple where his reputation grew so that it came to be a common proverb in Cilicia,. 'Whither hastenest thou—art going to the Youth?'

Even the God of the temple regarded him so favourably that when an Assyrian youth suffering from the results of intemperance came to the temple the Divinity sent him to Apollonius to be healed. The latter said to him, 'Speak not as if the God or I could give thee health, which comes only to those who desire or deserve it; but thou art working against thine own health.'

One of the wealthiest among the Cilicians offered in the temple sacrifices greater than had ever beeu received there, beseeching for the restoration of one of his eyes. On nearing of the case Apollonius advised the priests to have nothing to do with the man; saying that he seemed to be bribing the priests, rather than seeking favour of of the God; and the God himself appeared in the night commanding that the man should depart with all his presents for, said the vision, 'neither does he deserve to retain his other eye.'

One day Apollonius asked one of the priests, 'Are the Gods righteous?' 'Doubtless', was the response. 'Reasonable also?' 'Why, what could be more reasonable han Divinity!' 'And do they know the circumstances of men?' 'That is the very root of their Divinity, that they now all things', was the answer. 'If this all be so,' said Apollonius, 'it seems to me that the only prayer which a well-meaning person can pray is, *O ye Gods, give to me what is suitable to me.*'

The beauty of the youthful body of Apollonius became a temptation to the ruler of Cilicia, who came to the temple under the pretext of sacrificing to the God, but besought Apollonius to be his mediator on the ground of Apollonius' reputation of standing in the good graces of the Divinity—'Make the God friendly to me', pled he. But Apollonius answered, 'Why should you need that, if you are an honest man? The Gods glady accept honest persons without any mediator.' 'But,' said the governor, 'the God has publicly shown favour to you'. Apollonius answered, 'This is only so because Virtue recommended me to him; and because I have made virtue my life, so has he received me as servant and friend; let virtue with you also be a sufficient introduction to the Divinity.'

When Apollonius heard of the death of his father, he hastened to Tyana, and with his own hands buried him near the grave of his mother. The large estate he divided with his brother, who was a man given up to drink and already in the years of majority. Several years later, when he himself had come to be of age, he returned to Tyana; he found that his brother had persisted in his evil ways, and had lost much of his money. Many of his former friends suggested to him to reform his brother, but he said, 'How could I reform one older than I?'

Yet he did what he could; he gave to his brother the half of his own inheritance, saying that the brother needed more than he himself did. Then he spoke to him as follows: 'Our father has departed from us, and we lack his teaching and warning; we two are now alone in the world. Wherein I fail, instruct me; and I will return the favour.' Thus, as one tames wild horses through kindness, did Apollonius endeavour to move his brother thro' gentleness.

Having done what he could for his brother, he gave away the rest of his patrimony to the poorest among his relations, doing better than did Anaxagoras who in order to become poor gave up his patrimony to sheep and goats, or Crates, who sank his patrimony in the ocean.

It happened that somebody expressed before Apollonius admiration for those doctrines of Pythagoras which taught that a man should go to no woman other than his wife. Apollonius answered, 'I shall then never marry, nor seek the enjoyment of love.' Wherein he was greater even than Sophocles who said he had escaped from lust, as from a wild, raging master, after he had attained age; but Apollonius, protected by virtue and modesty, succumbed not, even as a youth, to this evil mastery, and ruled perfectly his less honourable members, even while he was yet strong in body.

Euxenus, seeing that his former pupil had attained much clearness of mind, asked him why he did not record his teachings in a book—to which Apollonius answered, 'Because I have not yet learned to keep still.' So he began a course of silence while his eyes and spirit laid up much knowledge in his memory, that faculty of his which remained active even to his extreme age, and seemed a marvel to all who knew him. During this silence the expression of his eye and the grace of his gesture so much attracted all to him that his silence almost became an added grace.

After this period of silence, he went to the temple of Apollo in Antioch. Here he began to teach publicly, and oft went to desert places 'since', said he, 'I seek not *males*, but *men*.' For any number of *males* can be found in cities, bnt to find *men* it is often necessary to search places of retirement.

After this beginning of public ministry he spent much time in various temples purifying the rites. He loved to converse with the priests early in the morning, 'for', said he, 'it is at the time of dawn that we must commune with the Gods.' He generally spoke in simple words, avoiding rhetoric and poetry, holding converse not only with the more educated and refined, but even with the most ignorant, if worthy.

It was about this time that he began to think of a distant voyage to India, so as to learn the wisdom of the Babylonians and Hindus. So he assembled his disciples and said to them: 'I have taken the Gods as counsellors, and have made a decision; I now desire to try you, to see whether you be strong enough for that for which I feel myself able; but as I see from your looks that most of you are not strong enough, so, farewell. I must go whither Wisdom and the Daemon within will lead me.' And so he left Antioch, accompanied only by the two slaves that did the one his slow, and the other his fast writing.

It was at Nineveh, where was a statue of Io, the daughter of Iacchus, that he met the Ninevite Damis, who remained his disciple faithfully to the end of his life. 'Let us go on, Apollonius; thou following the God, and I thee; besides, I will be useful as a guide, for I know all the languages of the country.' 'So do I ', answered Apollonius. 'How so?' 'Oh, I know all the languages inasmuch as I know what men do not care to express.'

While passing through Mesopotamia they were stopped at a toll-gate and the officers asked what he brought with him. Apollonius, employing the Greek terms which are all of the feminine gender, said, 'I bring with me

Moderation, Justice, Virtue, Abstemiousness, Manliness, and Endurance.' The toll-gate keeper, looking for much money, wrote them down as female slaves, but Apollonius said, 'That will not do; I bear with me not slaves, but mysteries.'

Passing beyond Etesiphon they were seized by soldiers and brought to the satrap at the very moment he was preparing to leave his tent. Suddenly seeing these foreign men he cried like a coward, and hid his face. Finally he said, 'Whence are you, and whither are you going? Apollonius answered, 'Sent by myself to you in the hope that I might perhaps, against your will, make a man of you.' 'But who are you who desire to visit the lands of the king?' 'The whole earth is mine,' retorted Apollonius, 'and I wander through it at will.' On mutual explanations the governor offered him money. and a safe-conduct to the king. Apollonius refused the money, but acceqted bread and fruits.

Warned by a vision, he went to a colony of Eretrians who had been colonized several hundred years before, but who were still being maltreated by their neighbours. He thus became familiar with their condition, and was later able to procure a mitigation of their sufferings by a decree of the king of Babylon, as the only present he would accept from the king.

On entering the great city of Babylon he refused to do reverence to the images of the king; and this having been brought to the ears of the governors, he was cited before them and asked why he despised the king. 'I have not scorned him,' said Apollonius. 'But would you do so?' 'Certainly,' declared Apollonius, 'if in personal relations with him I should find that he was not noble or honourable.' Asked what persons he brought with him he said, 'I bring with me Courage and Righteousness.' Asked whether he said that he brought them as intimating that the king lacked them, he answered, 'Nay, only that he may learn to use them, if he have them.'

He was brought before the king, and on the way while entering the magnificent palace he did not so much as look at it, but discoursed with Damis about the names of certain hymns of Homer. The king was in the act of sacrificing a white horse of the genuine Nisaic breed, and invited Apollonius to take part. But Apollonius refused, contenting himself with throwing a grain of incense on the fire, with these words: 'Send me, O celestial Sun, as far upon the earth as may seem suitable to thee and me, and bring it about that I may learn to know virtuous men, and that the evil may neither know me, nor I them.' Of his peculiar attire and doctrines he said, 'My wisdom is that of the Samian Pythagoras who taught me to serve the Gods in this manner, and to understand them, whether visible or invisible.'

The king invited him to dwell in the palace, but Apollonius refused because 'If I should dwell with persons above my social position, I would not be happy, for the wise man is oppressed by luxury more than the rich by need; let me dwell with some person who possesses as little wealth as I. But I will be with thee as much as thou mayest desire.'

The king insisted he should wish for ten things. Damis supposed that Apollonius would not ask for anything, inasmuch as his daily prayer was, *O ye Gods, grant me this, to have litte, and need nothing.* But he did not despise this opportunity, and pled for the Eretrian colonists, saying to Damis the he alone deserved a reward for abstemiousness who had refused to accept what he was proud of lacking.'

Damis said, 'I think that the Wise Man is pursued by dangers greater than than those of a sailor or a warrior; whatever he does, he is criticized for it.' 'Nor,' added Apollonius, 'because we are here in Babylon is our danger less; for think not that a sin committed here in Babylon is less than had it been committed in Athens or Olympia; for a Wise Man Hellas is everywhere, nor consider any land desert or barbarian, since he lives under the eyes of Virtue, who deigns to look but on few men.'

At the moment the herald came to summon him to
the king, Apollonius happened to be praying, and he answered, 'I will come when I have finished my business
with the Gods.'

While Appolonius stood before the king a eunuch,
caught with one of the king's concubines, was brought
in, dragged by his hair. The king desired Apollonius to
pass sentence upon him as he saw fit. Apollonius said,
'I condemn him to live.' 'How so?' said the king redd-
ening; 'does he not deserve punisment?' 'Oh yes,' said
Apollonius; 'life is the greatest punishment that he could
suffer, for if he continues to act out his passion he wil
be satisfied with nothing, he will not be able to sleep, he
will perish as from the plague. He will yet come some
day, O king, to beg thee for death, or he will kill himself, and curse the day on which he did not die.' Thus
mildly and wisely dealt Apollonius, and the king sancti-
oned his decision.

The king asked him how he might strengthen his government. The answer was, 'By honouring many, but
trusting few.'

The king happened to fall ill, and by his bedside A-
pollonius entertained him, discoursing concerning the
soul and immortality. The king lying on his bed drew a

long breath and said to his attendants, 'Apollonius removes from me care not only about the kingdom, but about death also.

On being shown by the king the walls of the city of Ekbatana, and being asked whether it was not a dwelling fit for the Gods, he answered, 'Certainly, a dwelling of the Gods; but whether it be a dwelling of men, I do not know. The city of the Lacedemonians has no walls.'

The king showed him the royal treasures, so as to awaken in him cupidity for money. He hardly looked at them. The king said, 'How may I best use all this?' 'By making use of it', was the apt rejoinder.

When the time of departure arrived, the only gift Apollonius would accept was that the king should reward reward his own wise men for their kind treatment of him, though accepting the necessary guide and camels for the journey to India. On being asked by the king what he proposed to bring back with him, Apollonius answered: 'A delightful present, O king; for if my intercourse with those men makes me wiser, so will I return to thee better than I am now.' With tears did the king embrace him, and said, 'May you only return to me—this will indeed be a great present!'

Phraotes

Riding on the camels furnished by the king, and led by the guides, Apollonius and Damis passed on through Media to the Himalaya Mountains, by them taken to be a further branch of the Kaukasus. The road led up on to the heights above the mists of the valley, where the sun seemed more splendid, and the stars clearer. The guides declared that this was the dwelling-place of the Gods. But Apollonius' mind was intent rather on the practical aspect of religion, and he asked Damis what difference had obtained since the day before. 'We are nearer Heaven,' answered the latter. 'But,' rejoined the former, 'dost thou now know more of spiritual things than thou knewest yesterday?' 'Nay, though the sky seem so near that I feel as if I could touch it with a stick.' 'Then art thou still below, and hast gained nothing through the height, and art as far from Heaven as yesterday, when we were passing through the plains. When thy soul shall unswervingly behold such things as *What is truth*, or *justice*, or *righteousness?* then wilt thou be far higher than even on these glorious mountains.'

Beyond the mountains they came again into the plains and passed many friendly tribes who presented to them, among other things, palm-wine, as they chanced to be resting near a clear spring of water. After the guides had refreshed themselves, Damis made a libation with the palm-wine, and offered some of it to Apollonius, on the plea that it was not really wine made of grapes, and would refresh him after so long a fast. But Apollonius laughingly refused, remarking that the palm-wine was to the Indian tribes as much wine as that of the grapes was to the Greeks. But he eucouraged the others to partake of it, himself abstaining on the ground that whereas abstemiousness might not profit them as with them it would be exceptional, yet it would profit himself as being the recognized, settled rule of his life 'by virtue of the Covenant I made with Philosophy from my early childhood'.

As they approached the Indus they met a boy riding on an elephant. This gave rise to a helpful conversation between the friends, in the course of which Apollonius related the strange legend that although captive elephants remain silent in the day-time while working under the discipline of man, yet at night, when they believe themselves alone, they lament for their early life of freedom before they were caught and tamed, with peculiar cries of misery. But should any human being quite unawares catch him doing this, the elephant was said suddenly to stop, as if ashamed of himself. Thus has even the elephant learnt to control himself.

Beyond the Indus they came to Taxila, the capital of India. While waiting in the temple until the king of the country should be told of their arrival, the friends admired the pictures in the temple, and, as usual, their conversation turned on the spiritual aspect of what they saw. 'God is a painter; and, stepping out of the winged chariot in the which flying He superintends all earthly and divine things, He made the beauties of nature like children playing in the sand.'

When introduced into the king's presence-chamber they found it so very simple that Apollonius greeted the king as a philosopher and asked whether such simplicity was the rule in that land, or if the king himself had introduced it? The king answered that he had still simplified the already remarkable traditional simplicity inasmuch as, though he possessed more than any other human being yet he needed but little—his great possessions he considered the property of his friends. For this speech Apollonius reverenced the king Phraotes, and all his life long referred to him as an example of moderation. The king further stated that he used no more wine than was necessary to sacrifice to the Sun. 'What game I catch

when hunting, I give to others, being satisfied with th
exercise I get while hunting. For food I am conten
with vegetables, palms, and grasses nurtured by the riv
er.' While hearing this, Apollonius looked approvingl
over to Damis.

Having motioned to the guard to withdraw, Phraote
came up to Apollonius and asked him, 'Would you reall
at home deign to accept me as a guest?' 'How so?' sai
the latter. 'Because,'-explained the king, 'I consider the
far better than myself;wisdom is greater than royal rank.
During the banquet the king related to Apollonius th
qualifications which a youth must in India possess be
fore being admitted to the career of philosophy. He mus
be eighteen years of age, and there must have been n
libertine, no criminal and no extortioner among his an
cestry up to the third generation. Then the youth him
self was tested: whether he have a good memory, be ab
stemious in eating and drinking, be neither boastful no
immodest, and have not misemployed the bloom of hi
youth. After this test only was a youth admitted to th
teachings of the Brahmins. At the close of the banque
arose a hymn accompanied by flute-playing. An ancien
custom demanded that every evening a sort of serenad
of good advice be given to the king, who said that h
permitted it to be continued out of regard for ancien

custom. As to the exhortations, he paid no heed to them because 'when a king does useful and helpful things he is serving himself even better than his subjects even.'

Next morning before dawn the king entered into the room allotted to Apollonius expecting to find him sleeping lightly 'for', said he, 'water-drinkers sleep indeed, but with a light sleep which, as one might say, rests on the eyes but not the soul'. Soberness and even-mindedness permit the water-drinker to sleep sweetly. And it is only the visions that come in the sleep of dawn that are actual, and not merely the results of intoxication. Water drinkers may in one sense be considered as possessed by the divinity, as being 'bacchantes of soberness'. The king asked, 'Will you make me such an one?' Apollonius answered, 'That must depend on your position as king. For a moderate and mild philosophy will produce just such a mellow, charming disposition as yours is; but the too serious attainments, often becoming exaggerated, usually lead to offence with the people—which for a public man gives rise to unpleasant circumstances.'

When Apollonius saw that the king's business demanded he should leave, he voluntarily suggested to the king that he himself desired to go into privacy according to his daily custom to worship the Sun. The grateful king answered 'May the Sun hear thy prayer, for in thus do-

ing it will send gladness into the hearts of all that love
thy wisdom.'

An ancient custom forbade strangers to abide anywhere
longer than three days; and soon Phraotes dismissed Apollonius with a commendatory letter to Iarchas, the lead-
er of the Brahmins Apollonius had come to visit; and i
began as follows: 'Apollonius, the wisest of men, con-
siders you wiser than himself, and comes to learn from
you. Dismiss him not, therefore, without a knowledge
of that which you know. Thus shall your wisdom no
be lost, for none speaks better or remembers better than
he.'

Is the world alive? 'Yes, if you mean that sensibly, since it endows all else with life.' Nature is not male or female, but both, as it produces and cherishes life. The world is, as It were, a ship; God is the commander, and the officers are the many divinities that rule the earth under The God, of whom there are many in the skies, on the earth, yea, some under the earth.

Damis was not entirely left out of the conversation, and Iarchas addressed him from time to time, in the course of an answer to one of which Damis explained the reasons why he had felt attracted to Apollonius when he had first met nim; he was wise, strong and thoughtful, and possessed self-mastery and a good memory. These are surely not small recommendations.

The conversation touched on all arts and sciences, the geography and natural history of the country, 'prophecy, and divination by consideration of the stars. In such daily intercourse four months passed rapidly, when Apollonius decided to return home. The Brahmins accompanied him a little ways prophesying that not only after his death, but even before he should be reverenced as a Divinity. And even after turning back from accompanying him as long as he was in sight they ever turned back to look at him, in proof that it was only in sorrow that they parted from him.

BOOK THIRD

The Brahmins

The Brahmins resided beyond the Ganges on a mountain which might be compared to the Akropolis of Athens, rising from a valley with rocks around its summit, which was generally hid by clouds. Here dwelt the sages in calmness and silence, exercising many spiritual gifts such as foresight, among others. In later years Apollonius ever described them thus: 'I saw the Indian Brahmins who live on the earth and not on the earth; in a citadel, without fortifications; without property, and yet in possession of all things.'

Apollonius was greeted by the sages, who led him to their chief, Iarchas. The latter, as being the senior, did not rise from his iron throne, distinguished from the rest by golden ornaments. As warrant of his attainments Iarchas greeted Apollonius by recounting to him his former life in its minutest details and conversations. Apollonius, marvelling, asked him whence he had this knowledge? 'Thou thyself comest to us endowed with this wisdom; but not yet with all that thou shalt have.' 'And wilt thou teach me all wisdom?' 'Certainly, for this is wiser

Apollonius returned home not the way he had come, but by the ocean, the ship passing the mouths of the Indus, Patala, the island Byblos famous for shell-fish, Pegada the land of iron rocks, Stobera the city of the fish-eaters, Balara the city of myrtle and laurel forests, and the island Salera, the home of pearls. Thus were the mouths of the Euphrates reached, whence they sailed up to Babylon where they again met their old friend king Bardanes; and then through Nineveh, Seleucia, Cyprus and Paphos to Ionia.

BOOK FOURTH

The First Labours in Greece.

Apollonius' return to the Hellenic world aroused the greatest interest in his teaching and reverence for his person. Oracles spoke of him, and commanded the sick to go to him for healing; his features, strength, and habits riveted the attention of everybody. Cities sent him embassies for counsel in building temples, and in difficult decisions. From Smyrna came an invitation to come 'to see and be seen.' He answered, 'I shall come, and may you, O Muses, grant it to me that we may also learn to love each other.'

He did not employ the indirect Socratic method in his preaching; he exhorted his hearers directly, as for instance the Ephesians, that they should abandon the pursuit of pleasure, and devote themselves instead to that of knowledge and wisdom. Nor did he hesitate because the pleasure-loving crowds were thereby antagonized. He persisted in this course, winning his hearers by his marvellous gifts of oratory and foresight as for instance when once preaching about the desirability of, and duty to assist each other he took as an example a number of birds

‷ were summoned to a lucky find of corn by a fellow-
‷row who had discovered it.

‷e found the Smyrnaeans devoted to study, and he
‷rted them to persevere in this course, encouraging
‷m to pay more attention to themselves than to the ex-
‷or of their city. For buildings remain stationary, but
‷ured men will spread the reputation of the city while
‷elling. On seeing that there were political divisions in
‷ city Apollonius recommended *good discord*, not one
‷ should bear the fruit of civil war, but a praiseworthy
‷test as to who could best do their duty by, or give
‷ best advice to the city government.

‷While here he was called back to Ephesus where the
‷gue which he had in part foreseen and prophesied, but
‷hout being able to make the citizens take precaution-
‷ measures, had broken out. He stayed the plague by
‷embling the people in the theatre, and by stoning an
‷d beggar in spite of the better feelings of the crowd.
‷was said, however, that when the stones were remov-
‷it was found that the remains were not those of a hu-
‷n being but of a demon, dog-like in shape, foaming
‷he mouth. Whether this be a story due to Damis, or
‷, is of course unascertainable—but it is a story which
‷ that of the Gadarene swine, one wishes were not
‷sent. The plague was however stayed, and a statue

to Herakles the Protector erected on the spot.

On the way to Greece he passed through Pergamos, and on the last day of his stay there he commanded his companions to take ship leaving him alone that he might visit the tomb of Acchilles to hold communion with the latter. In the morning many persons crowded on the ship, desiring to take passage to Greece on it, being persuaded that Apollonius had power over storms. To accomodate them he took passage on a larger ship. They touched at Lesbos where he erected a statue and temple to Palamedes the hero of the Trojan war. He also visited the temple of Orpheus. On the passage Damis insisted on hearing what Achilles had told him—which after all regarded only some details of the Trojan war. For the season of the year the voyage to the Piraeus was a most fortunate one, besides being a most agreeable one.

It was one of the last days of the Eleusinian mysteries, the day of the Epidaurians. The arrival of Apollonius created such a stir that many candidates for the Mysteries neglected them in order to see something of him. On hearing of this Apollonius exhorted the latter to return to the Mysteries; and in order to persuade them declared that with them he would also seek initiation. But the Hierophant refused him admittance on the ground that he was a magician, and defiled by intercourse with

demons. But Apollonius said, 'I came to be initiated by
a man wiser than I, but I see I know more about the
Mysteries than you do.' Afraid of the crowd, the Hierophant changed his mind, but Apollonius refused, prophesied that he should be initiated four years later, when
another priest should be in charge, whom he named. He
then philosophized about the right manner of offering
sacrifices to the Gods, but was interrupted by the laughter of a sybaritic youth, out of whom Apollonius drove
a demon, leaving him modest, gentle, ready to philosophize. He further corrected the Dionysiac dances and
the gladiatorial games before he left Athens for Thessaly,
in order to carry out the instructions of Achilles. These
he delivered to the Thessalians assembled at the Amphy-
ktonian games at Pylaea, whence he proceeded to Ther-
mopylae, visiting the spot where Leonidas was said to
have died. Hearing his followers discuss which was the
highest mountain in Greece, he called them to himself
and said, 'This is the highest mountain in Greece; for
those who died here elevated it even above Olympos.'

It was in Corinth that Demetrius the philosopher sent
some of his disciples to Apollonius to learn of him, as of
a light greater than himself. Among these disciples was
the man who was entrapped by the Lamia, a beautiful
woman who turned out to have been a serpent in dis-

guise when Apollonius forced her to reveal her true nature, and that of her gold and banquet-appointments. At
about the same time the Ephors at Lacedaemon sent to
invite him to their city by messengers clothed so sybarit-
ically that he wrote them back a sharp rebuke about it.

In Olympia Apollonius preached often, about his old
subjects—wisdom, courage, abstemiousness and all the o-
ther virtues. Therefore the Lacedaemonians were ready
to celebrate in his honour the ceremonies of a Theopha-
ny, receiving him as a God; but Apollonius withdrew,
to avoid giving grounds for envy and jealousy. It was
while here that a touching incident occurred. A youth,
a descendant of Kallikratidas the Lacedaemonian admiral
was so interested in the traditional nautical interests of
his family that he did not attend to his public duties.
Hearing of this Apollonius voluntarily went to him and
persuaded him to change his ways, brought him to the
Ephors, and obtained his pardon..

In the spring Apollonius went to Malea so as to take
passage for Rome, but was in a dream warned first to go
to Crete For this he chose a ship large enough to hold
all his immediate followers, calling both his companions
and their slaves his *congregation*—'for he did not neglect
even these slaves.'

Finally, however, Apollonius arrived in Italy, and
went Romewards as far as the Arician grove, where he
met the philosopher Philolaos who had fled from Rome
at Nero's persecutions against the philosophers. Although
Apollonius expressed himself as full of courage, and as
despising an emperor who behaved so foolishly, yet Philolaos in a loud voice insisted on the great danger he
would incur. Damis remonstrated with him, and warned
him that his disciples would be frightened. But Apollonius only said, 'This will be a valuable means of testing
which of them are true philosophers, and which of them
have other purposes in view.' And out of thirty-four
disciples twenty-six left for various reasons—one that he
had had bad dreams; the other that he lacked money,
another that he was sick and longed for home. Only
eight remained faithful to philosophy. These Apollonius
called together and spoke to them earnestly and encour-
agingly, assuring them of his protection under the Gods.

So they entered the gates of Rome, and sought lodg-
ing in an inn near by. While there, there came in a
strolling player who sang some of Nero's songs, who
according to his custom demanded a contribution under
pains of persecuting the listeners for public contempt of
the emperor. Menippus asked Apollonius what he
thought of the fellow's conduct—'As little as I do of

his sinning' was the characteristically Apollonian answer.
Nevertheless, to avoid needless trouble the money was
paid.

By dawn of next day Telesinus, one of the consuls,
had Apollonius called before him to inquire of his teaching. 'It is reverence for the Gods, and knowledge of the
right manner of worshipping them.' What prayest thou
when thou comest to the altar? 'I pray as follows: *May
Justice reign, may the laws not be broken, may the wise
men be poor, and the poor men rich, without sin.*' And
when you pray to the Divinities for great things, do you
expect to receive them? 'Certainly, for I recapitulate all
prayers in one: *O ye Gods, grant me that which is fit-
ting unto me.*' 'For if I am good, then will I receive
more than I desire; and if I be evil I will lack deserved-
ly.' So Telesinus gave his written permission that Apollonius dwell in the temples, both those in the city and
neighbourhood, and Apollonius travelled around freely
from the one to the other, as the spirit moved him.

It chanced that about this time Demetrius was in
Rome teaching. Now it chanced that Nero dedicated the
New Baths, and Demetrius publicly found fault with
them as a public waste of money. The only reason Nero did not execute him was that Nero was so pleased because he was in good voice that day. But Demetrius was

iven from Rome and the publicly acknowledged friend-
ip between the exile and Apollonius brought the latter
disfavour. Moreover, on the occasion of an eclipse,
pollonius declared in public that great things would ta-
place, and would not take place. Three days later
er Nero's cup was cast out of his hand by lightning,
d Tigellinus the prefect was so terrified at Apollonius'
ident foreknowledge of events that although he dared
t oppose him directly, lest Apollonius use his supposi-
ious magic power against him, yet he had him spied
on continually.

It so chanced that about this time a slight epidemic of
ugh and catarrh raged in Rome affecting the emperor's
 nging voice temporarily. Soon the temples were filled
ith suppliants praying the Gods for Nero's voice.
hough disgusted, Apollonius said nothing, and persuad-
Menippus to do likewise, though saying to him he
ould never forgive the Gods if they should grant such
olish prayers. This speech was made the ground of an
cusation, on account of which he was cited before Ti-
llinus and asked what was his business and reason for
avelling. 'In order to get to know God, and to under-
and myself and other men, it being more difficult to
ow himself than other men.' Why dost thou not fear
ero? 'Because the God who gave it to Nero to be te-

rrible has given it to me to be unterrified.' And Tigellinus said, 'Go where thou wilt—thou art stronger than
that I had power over thee.'

Shortly before his departure from Rome Apollonius
performed a deed that attracted general notice. A young
bride died on the day of her marriage.. Apollonius met
the funeral procession, stopped it, asked for her name,
spoke to her in a low tone of voice, and caused her to
become reanimated. The large sum that her relatives offered Apollonius as a reward he added to the girl's marri-
age-portion. Damis is not sure whether the girl had been
entirely dead or only in a trance; in any case, she was
given back to life, to the joy of herself, and the whole
city.

FIFTH BOOK

The Second Labours in Greece

It was not long before Apollonius and his disciples left
Rome to travel through Spain, the northern provinces of
Africa and Sicily, from whence he took ship for Greece.
Landing in Athens he was initiated by the very hierophant whose name he had predicted four years earlier.
Here he found Demetrius living and teaching in compar-
ative security, whereas, in passing by the Isthmian canal
Apollonius had recognized among the convict labourers
working on it his friend the philosopher Musonius whom
he had met at Rome. Seeing him, Apollonius tried to at-
tract his attention. The latter, however, said nothing,
and only hit the harder with his pick-axe. But he changed his mind, stopped, looked up and said 'You are dis-
tressed at seeing me work on the Isthmus here; what
would you say if you saw me playing the guitar, like
Nero?'

The next few months were spent in Greece visiting
temples and cities and, as Damís has taken pains to state,
not condemning everything, for when he found things he
approved of, he did not hesitate to praise it. On arriving

to the Piraeus he found a ship ready to sail; but the owner refused to take him on the plea that his cargo of statues of the Gods ought not to be defiled by the careless conversation of chance passengers. Consequently they chose another ship—or rather, he chose one, and his friends sprang in after him, 'for his friends showed their wisdom especially in this that they followed in his footsteps.' So they all finally reached Rhodes, famous for its Pharos. On catching sight of it the marvelling Damis asked Apollonius if he knew of anything greater? 'Certainly! The man who with healthy and unsophisticated mind practices the wisdom he possesses.'

It chanced that there was at that time in Rhodes a young man who had suddenly fallen heir to great wealth. He had built himself a house and being very proud of it insisted on showing it to Apollonius. But the latter asked him how much he had spent on his own education, and how much on his house. The answer was, nothing on himself, but on the house twelve talents—nay, perhaps twice that amount. 'What is the purpose of this house?' 'To be a splendid abode for my body, that men may admire me on account of my riches.' 'But tell me—which are better able to take care of their riches, the cultured or the uncultured?' As the youth remained silent Apollonius continued, 'It would almost seem as if it was not o owned the house, but as if the house owned

wise he met a corpulent youth who prided him-
the amount he ate and drank. Apollonius asked,
good results hast thou from thy gluttony?' 'That
marvel at me, and I become famous; for even
es is famous not only for his works, but also for
els he ate.' But Apollonius retorted, 'Ah yes, be-
e was Herakles, and was virtuous; but, O worth-
ow, what is the virtue in thee?'

en Apollonius approached Alexandria, which had
r loved him, and yearned exceedingly for his pre-
the crowds that met him were very great. It hap-
that just as he was entering the gates of the city
met by the sad procession of ten criminals being
o execution. He begged the guards to go as slow-
ey well could, and to delay the execution, as one
n was innocent. And indeed, as they had cut off
eads, there came a rider with the news of the re-
of one of them, by name Pharion, who, though
at, had confessed under torture. This deed earned
ollonius great reverence.

praised the ritual of the Egyptian temples, but
ault with the bloodiness of their sacrifices, point-
that prognostication was as possible from the

melting of an image of incense as from the slaying of
bulls and geese. He also reproved their passion for horse
racing which often led to bloodshed.

Vespasian's first desire, on visiting Alexandria, was to
converse with Apollonius, and he went to meet him in
the temple, saying to him, 'Make me emperor.' Apollonius answered, That is what I made thee; for in that I
prayed for an emperor who should be just, noble, pater-
nal and moderate, did I pray for thee.' Vespasian grateful and delighted, exclaimed, 'May it be given to me to
rule over wise men, and may wise men ever rule over
me!' Next morning, at dawn, Apollonius went to Vespasian's palace and asked the guard what the emperor
might happen to be doing at the time. 'He has been up
long since already, and is now writing letters.' Whe-
reat Apollonius turned round to Damis, saying, 'That
man will yet rule the empire.' When, later in the day,
he was admitted to Vespasian's presence, he exhorted
the latter to permit the admittance of Euphrates and Di-
on, two philosophers who were jealous of Apollonius'
success with Vespasian and the people. Vespasian answered, 'My door is always open to wise men; but to
thee is even my breast open.' They talked of the evil
lives of the late emperors, Apollonius remarking, 'Thou
art like the flute-player who sent his son for instruction

poor flute-players, in order to learn how not to play the flute. The same hast thou done.'

After much consultation Vespasian asked Apollonius to teach him to rule as a good prince should. 'You ask something impossible. It cannot be taught—it must be acquired. Yet see to it that wealth seem to thee not too important, nor the money that is forced from the poor, all tarnished with their tears. Fear above all the freedom to do as thou pleasest. Let the law rule thee also, O Emperor; thou wilt give wiser laws, if thou do not despise them. Consider the imperial power not so much as an inherited property, as a reward of virtue.' And when Apollonius desired to travel further inland, and so leave Vespasian, the latter asked him if he would not remember him in love? 'Certainly,' replied the sage, 'if thou remainest a good ruler, and remainest conscious of thy better self.'

It was at this time that there arose the difficulty between Apollonius and Euphrates that was to become so fatal for the former. For although Euphrates had advised Vespasian to establish a democracy when he should have dethroned Vitellius, yet when Vespasian invited the philosophers to ask him for some gift, Euphrates asked for what amounted to much money, while Apollonius refused everything. Euphrates had written his requests in a

letter, hoping that Vespasian would read it privately; but
the latter being incensed at Euphrates' private defamation
of Apollonius determined to read it publicly, to the a-
musement of all, Apollonius joining in the laughter and
twitting him with his former advice of democracy as the
best form of government. Henceforward Euphrates became his mortal enemy, and left no stone unturned to
injure Apollonius.

On determining to go into the innermost of Egypt,
Apollonius left behind him his disciple Dioskorides as
too weak for the journey, and also Menippus to watch
Euphrates; and once more he gave his disciples, who a-
gain amounted to thirty, the opportunity of staying in
place of risking the unknown dangers and privations of
the journey. Of these thirty twenty were frightened at
the prospective danger; but Apollonius with his remain-
ing ten disciples set sail for the Upper Nile.

The Gymnosophists

The little party sped safely up the Nile to the very
confines of Ethiopia. Here they found by the roadsides,
unwatched, large quantities of gold, ivory, roots and spi-
ces which had been left there by the Ethiopians (so honest was everybody there) until the merchants should, on
their yearly trip, come to exchange these goods for the
manufactures of Egypt.. This honesty and simplicity
made a deep impression on Apollonius who in his mind
compared it with the mercenariness and discord among
the Greeks. 'Ah, would God,' cried he, 'that as much
as here among the Greeks wealth were valueless, that
equallty should bloom, and that the iron sword lay far
away!'

As they were sailing up the Nile they met a bark
steered by a youth by name Timasion who seeing the sages clad in foreign garb and studying books called out to
them that he begged for the privilege of leading them up
the Nile, on the ground that he loved philosophy. Apollonius granted the request; and after the change had been
made he asked the boy to give some account of his life;

but Timasion blushed, and kept silence. Now Apollonius, by his gift of foresight, had, on first seeing him, told
his disciples Timasion's whole life-story, which was remarkable in its way. A child of rich parents, he had abandoned his home, and undertaken the life of a boatman, rather than yield to the solicitations of his blooming
young step-mother. And finally he confessed that this
was so, and he was praised for his modesty and courage.

Near the sanctuary of Memnon they met one who had
killed a man unwittingly, but whom the Gymnosophists
had so far failed to purify, so that for the time being he
was hopelessly exiled in the wilderness. Apollonius purified him according to the Greek manner, and sent him
home in peace.

They found the Gymnosophists by no means friendly,
for Euphrates had forestalled them by sending Thrasyboulos to prepossess them against Apollonius by various
arts, so that though they did not exactly refuse to receive
him, nevertheless they pretended they were too busy to
do so, pretending to desire to know first, before considering the matter, who he was. Apollonius, on the contrary, answered that he was surprised that they asked
him what he wanted; that the sages of India had not
done so, as their foresight had given them full instruction
in the matter. Damis, in talking over the matter with

Timasion, who had piloted Thrasyboulos, guessed that
Euphrates was at the bottom of the trouble, and Timasion was enabled to arrange for an interview.

Nilus, the youngest of the Gymnosophists, came and
invited Apollonius to a conversation in a grove. When
they had all assembled Thespesion, the oldest, took up
the parable, vaunting the abstemiousness of the Egyptian
philosophy in comparison with the Hindu love of pleasure. Apollonius responded by setting forth the require-
ments of the Pythagorean philosophy, insisting much on
the bridling of the tongue, and the drinking of water,
and many other austerities. 'If however,' continued he,
'those who have undertaken this mode of life shall show
themselves persistent, this is the result of it which I can
promise to them: Wise conduct and innate justice, with
envy towards none; to be more terrible to tyrants than
they can ever be to you; to be more welcome to the
Gods with small sacrifices than those who shed the blood
of oxen. Thus purified shall my disciple attain foresight;
and his eyes shall be so filled with rays of light that he
shall recognize Gods and Heroes, and he shall be able to
discern evil spirits even when they assume human form.'
When he reached the sages of India, said he, he had a
feeling such as the Athenians experienced when the tra-
gedies of Æschylos were for the first time represented:

'for I saw men who dwelt on earth, but did not live on it; who were surrounded by walls, without walls; and who though poor possessed all things.' Thespesion was struck with the power and spirituality of his philosophy, and begged pardon for his former treatment of Apollonius inviting the latter to recount his experiences in India.

After this, when Apollonius and his disciples had retired to eat their meal, Nilus came to them bringing slight presents, saying, 'I come not uninvited, for I invite myself.' Apollonius answered, 'You bring a present than which there could be none more delightful, yourself and your earnest good intentions.' Nilus decided to cast in his lot henceforth with Apollonius, who warned him not to act rashly; but Nilus declared that it was not a rash decision, inasmuch as he had uuited himself with the Gymnosophists solely for the truth that they might have; and that it was the same loyalty to truth which now, for a fuller form of it, forced him to leave them. Apollonius then accepted him, though on the condition that he pay the necessary reward. This Nilus promised to do, and asked what it was. Then Apollonius answered, 'The reward that I expect from thee is this, that thou shalt be content with that which thou hast chosen; and that thou shalt not burden the Gymnosophists with advice that might not be pleasant to them.'

'ell and good,' answered Nilus, 'I will follow thee,
are agreed about the reward.' .

The next day Apollonius asked to learn of the wisdom
the Gymnosophists. The first question he asked was
y the Egyptians worshipped the Divinities under such
rading forms as those of animals, contrasting with this
elevating Greek statues and pictures. Nilus answered
h much point, 'And have Phidias and Praxiteles as-
ded into heaven that they should the rather know
at the Gods look like?' While the Greeks honour the
ds by fancy, rather than by direct imitation, the E-
ptians did so symbolically, meaning much the same
ng. Apollonius propounded to them the same questi-
he had propounded to the sages of India, whether a
tain action of his in one of his former incarnations had
n just, because it had been not-unjust. It seems that
had been a pilot and had been caught by pirates who
made him swear to deliver into their hands the valua-
cargo he was to steer; but he managed both to fulfil
oath technically, yet he saved the cargo. Thespesion
eed with the Hindu sages that there was a difference
ween them.

They philosophized further about the
l and immortality, when regretfully they said farewell
each other, Timasion and Nilus leading the little par-

ty up the Nile to find its sources. They succeeded
reaching the third cataract whose noise was, said the
so great that it caused deafness—temporary, probabl
They did not proceed further up, claiming that a moun
ain eight stadii high was the source. and that the road
to it was impracticable. They returned downwards
Ethiopia.

One night they rested in a large village, and whi
they were pleasantly conversing a great noise arose ou
side of mingled cries of pain, and shouting. It seer
that for ten months a satyr had infested the place, mu
dering two women. Apollonius, remembering how Mi
as was said to have acted in such a case gave the Sat
wine to drink, whereupon he fell asleep, and thencefo
ward ceased from his evil ways. Damis distinctly mak
a point of it that this was not a chance deed of Apoll
nius', but a deed which he believed in some way
have been one of the main deeds of the journey.

Having returned to Alexandria the difficulties wi
Euphrates grew apace—Apollonius himself having litt
to do with him, Menippus and Nilus championing t
cause of Apollonius.

It was about this time that Alexandria heard the ne
that Titus had taken Jerusalem, and conquered the Jew
but had refused the crown which the neighbouring pe

ple had offered him. 'For,' he was reported to have said, 'it was not I who did this; it was the Divinity, to whom I loaned my hands as instruments.' Apollonius was so much pleased at this modesty and moderation that he sent to Titus by Damis the following letter: 'Since you do not desire to be feasted on account of the battle, and of the amount of blood of the enemies that you have shed, do I hereby reach unto you the crown of moderation. For you know what kind of a crown is alone worth having————Farewell!' Titus was pleased with the letter, and answered as follows: 'I have conquered Jerusalem, but thou hast conquered me.' Titus and Apollonius soon met in Greece, and renewed their pleasant exchange of good-will.

At the end of this meeting Titus asked Apollonius what he advised in respect to the art of ruling well. Apollonius answered: 'I shall advise you to do what you advise yourself, forasmuch as, since you love and obey your father Vespasian, it is evident that you will become similar to him.' And in parting, Apollonius spoke as follows: 'May you ever overcome your enemies with your weapons, and overcome your Father with virtues.' In response to Titus' request, he indicated Demetrius as a philosopher worthy of being imperial adviser to Titus when the latter should return Romewards.

A pleasant incident occurred at Tarsus, though it had
formerly been ill-disposed to Apollonius in consequence
of its once having been characterized by him *s giver
up to pleasure, and of its inability to accept this rebuke
in the helpful sense it was intended. It seems that the
city of Tarsus had an important request to make of Titus
and that the latter had answered that he himself was favourably inclined towards it, but would first consult his
father Vespasian. But Apollonius stood forth and asked
him what he, Titus, would do to a man who openly
raised rebellion against him? The answer was, Immediate
death. Then Apollonius asked, 'Does it not seem unfair
to execute punishment immediately, but to delay rewards?' Titus, appreciating the spirit of the rejoinder,
granted the request immediately.

Apollonius travelled further among the Hellenic races,
in Egypt, and Italy; and, says Damis, 'nowhere did he
neglect to appear worthy of himself. For, although it be
considered difficult to know oneself, yet is it still more
difficult for a sage to remain worthy of himself. But never can a sage improve or alter sinful persons until he
have first successfully practiced altering himself.

Amidst the chief events of this period are these.

He once found a comely youth of rich parentage who
spent his time teaching birds how to talk Greek, though

he himself spoke it only indifferently well. Apollonius told him that he was effecting two evils, spoiling the
natural song of the birds, and teaching them bad Greek.
Being rich, he would certainly become the prey of syco-
phants, who would ruin him unless he learned, at least,
how to defend himself in court efficiently. Had he been
younger, Apollonius would have advised him to give
himself up to philosophy; but at his age the study of
eloquence was the best he could do. The youth followed his advice.

A man advanced in age had four daughters, but possessed only twenty thousand drachmas which would give
each only a small dower, while leaving him penniless. So
he asked Apollonius for help, who after prayer advised
him to buy an olivegarden in which the man subsequent-
ly found a large sum of money hidden, the trees themselves yielding rich fruit in a season of famine, rendering
him wealthy and happy.

In Knydos there was a youth who had fallen in love
with the statue of naked Venus, and intended to marry
her. Hearing of this, Apollonius resolved to stop this—
not openly, to the hurt both the city and the youth—but
by-persuasion. He effected this by convincing him that
equals only should love each other; whereby the youth
was reclaimed from insanity, and restored to utility.

Domitian, not realising the full effect his order might have, ordained that no males should be castrated, and that no vines should be planted anew, nor the old ones be permitted to grow. This would have devastated the East. Apollonius encouraged the Eastern cities to send a petition to the Emperor, who ultimately rescinded his order.

Tarsus was once again the scene of a beautiful deed. A young man while exercising in the suburbs of the city was bitten by a dog. Supposing the dog to be mad, for thirty days he raged as if he himself had been a dog, recognizing none and frothing at the mouth. On hearing of the case Apollonius had Damis go and fetch the dog, who was not so much mad as terrified at the treatment he had undergone; he laid himself down at the feet of Apollonius, and groaned piteously. Then the young man was fetched, and the dog made to lick the wounds; and the youth, seeing that the dog was not mad, recovered. As for the dog, in order to assure his life, Apollonius after patting him and praying to the river-god, drove him through it; and after reaching the opposite bank the dog finding himself well, lay back his ears, wagged his tail and barked joyously, as if thanking Apollonius for saving his life.

Such were the gracious deeds Apollonius did.

SEVENTH BOOK

The Duel with Domitian

Damis begins this book with an account of the manner in which, at various times, philosophers have behaved when attacked by irresponsible tyrannical power, in order to illustrate the manner in which Apollonius dealt with Domitian 'so as to conquer him, rather than to be conquered by him.' This forms as it were a Greek 'Book of Martyrs'; an exhilarating record of what man can do to assert his individuality by no other means than moral power, unsupported by any 'supernatural revelation', resting on nothing but the divinely natural dignity of a worthy character, telling the truth not for the sake of either duty or rewards, but for its own sake. Zeno, Plato, Phyto, Heraklides and Pytho, Kallisthenes, Diogenes of Synope, Krates of Thebes—all these in their day asserted themselves against tyranny. But it was always tyranny over some petty state or island, not tyranny over the whole known world as in the case of Apollonius. Nor was Apollonius cowardly. What he said, he said openly, *coram populo*. Nor did he indulge his feelings in personalities; he confined himself to solemn

assertions of principle, the application of which to cu
rent events, if there was any, he always left to inference
only. For instance, when news came to Ephesus th
Domitian had executed three unchaste Vestal Virgias, h
cried out before the assembled multitude, 'O Helio
mayest thou also be freed from having to behold the u
just murders with which the world is filled at present

The circumstances which led up to Apollonius' diffi
ulties were as follows. While Domitian reigned, it seem
ed as if, after Domitian, Nerva, Orfitus, or Rufus we
destined to become emperor. Consequently Domitiah b
nished them—Nerva being sent to Tarentum. It so hap
pened that Apollonius was teaching by the banks of t
river Meles in Smyrna; and while standing by the ir
statue of Domitian he desired to impress his hearers wi
the powers of Fate, knowing as he did through his for
sight that Nerva should succeed Domitian as empero
So he cried out, 'O fool, how little understandest the
the Furies and Necessity! The man who is destined
reign after thee, though thou kill him, will resuscitate
None understood to which of the three Apollonius r
ferred; but Euphrates informed Domitian on Apolloniu
Domitian, to make sure of the right one, proposed
kill all three; but in order to lend some colour of justi
to the matter, he proposed to call Apollonius to accou

or his secret communications with these three men, as
Apollonius had kept up friendly relations with that fami-
y ever since he had first met Vespasian.

Now while Domitian was planning this, and, in fact,
while he was writing to the governor of Asia in the mat-
er, Apollonius, by his foresight, became aware of Domitian's plans. So he told his friends that he must make
a secret journey, without telling even to Damis what he
was resolved on. Immediately he took ship by Corinth
o Dikaearchia, an Italian port. Here he found his friend
Demetrius, again in exile. They embraced each other af-
fectionately, and Demetrius invited Apollenius to go with
him to the country in order to talk to each other privately. So they went to the former country-seat of Cicero,
where, under the plane-trees, the cicadas sang their rus-
tic songs. Addressing them, Apollonius revealed his business, and Demetrius rejoined, 'Sokrates was accused because he corrupted the youth and introduced new Gods;
but against us the accusation runs: He is punishable, because he is wise and just, knows Gods, men, and much
about laws.' Then Demetrius proceeded to tell Apollonius the exact charges advanced against him—that he had
been the prime mover of the ambition of three exiled
imperial aspirants; and that in their interests he had once
for the purposes of omination sacrificially slain a child.

And the fact that he had come to Italy before having received notification that he was wanted would only increase the suspicions of the tyrant that the imputation of magic was true. Demetrius advised him to take, while it was yet time, one of the ships in the harbor and flee to some distant foreign nation—'tyranny is less hard on excellent men when they live less excellently.'

Apollonius refused to flee on account of two reasons. First, he did not propose to be untrue to his friends, in betraying their confidence in him—inasmuch as to withdraw oneself from justice, however unjust it may really be, would be to condemn oneself; he would not be able to go to any of his friends; for if he did, he would have to do one of two things, both of which were against his principles: either to justify himself, or to accuse himself. Secondly, were he to flee, he would be untrue to himself, inasmuch as, having done something unworthy of his better self, nowhere that he would go would he be at peace with himself, nor could he any more pray to the Gods with a free conscience—it would drive him away from the temples, and from prayer.

Sadly did Demetrius assent to these principles; and he invited Apollonius to stay with him a few days. But Apollonius answered that this might needlessly bring suspicion—additional—on Demetrius; 'when I am vindicaed, then shall we eat together. Nay, come not even with me to the port; lest you be accused of conspiring with me.' And so Demetrius left him, with tears in his eyes, ever looking back until he was out of sight.

According to what was his custom when beginning a course more risky than usual, Apollonius turned to Damis and said, 'We have many times before this faced danger together; but it is yet time for you to stay here and avoid this serious crisis, if you are afraid.' 'How could I,' replied Damis with tears, 'after what I have heard thee say to-day about the community of dangers, and the faithfulness we owe our friends?' 'You are right,' answered Apollonius; 'come with me. But before you do so change your Pythagorean garments for usual ones, lest this difference of garments bring you also into needless difficulties.' So Damis changed his garments—out of obedience and wisdom, not out of cowardliness.

On the third day the ship reached the mouth of the Tiber. At that time it was Ælianus who 'held the sword' of the Emperor—in other words was the praefect of the praetorium. He was friendly to Apollonius, having loved Apollonius long since. In fact, even before Apollonius arrived he used what arts he could with the Emperor in his favour. He insisted that the sophists as a class had little that was enjoyable in life and consequently were su

. foolish as to seek death voluntarily, and that this accoun-
ted for their perpetual disturbances, and that the best
thing to do to annoy them was to pay no attention to
them; that this had been the reason why formerly Nero
had not executed Apollonius, considering it beneath his
dignity thus really to satisfy the sophist.

As soon as the latter arrived Ælianus did better still.
He had him immediately arrested and brought before
him. For, while apparently treating him with indignity,
he thus found an opportunity of speaking privately with
Apollonius, without raising any suspicion of his intentions. And when he had had him brought into the audi-
ence room that was private he told him' why he loved
him; because when in youth he was a chiliarch (captain)
in the army of Vespasian at the time the latter consulted
him at Alexandria. It seems that while the Emperor had
attended to business Apollonius had taken Ælianus aside,
told him his business and parentage, and prophesied to
him that he should hold this office; one which seemed to
most people a very exalted honour, but for which he almost despised himself. Apollonius answered pleasantly,
telling him he had not fled, as he easily could have done,
both on account of his friends who might have been
punished on account of their former connection with him
and his own lack of self-consistency should he flee.

Ælianus told Apollonius that the Emperor's frame of
[m]ind towards him was as that of a man who seeks to
[pu]nish, but as yet has no adequate reason for doing so;
[that] such punishment would give Domitian a legal pretext
[to] reach Nerva—that the main accusation against Apollo-
[ni]us was, in fact, that he had encouraged Nerva's aspir-
[at]ions to the throne by the omination of the sacrifice of
[th]e boy, at night, by waning moon, in the country. 'Thy
[sp]eech must not betray any scorn of the Emperor.' As
[so]on as he was confident that Apollonius was prepared
[fo]r the worst, and would not lose his composure even
[u]nder the severest trials, he said farewell tenderly; assu-
[m]ing anger, he called for the guard and bade him watch
[A]pollonius till the Emperor should call for him.

Among the greatest of the pains of being a prisoner
[w]as the petty humiliation which the lower officers sup-
[p]osed they were at liberty to heap on him. So one of
[th]e chiliarchs out of scorn demanded of Apollonius on
[a]ccount of what accusation might he be a prisoner? On
[A]pollonius' asseveration that he did not know, the chili-
[ar]ch said, 'I know, however; it is because people wor-
[sh]ipped you, and hold you to be a God.' 'And who ev-
[e]r worshipped me in that manner?' asked Apollonius.
['Why, I have done so myself !' answered the chiliarch,
['I]t was at the time when I was a child at Ephesus when

the city was delivered from the plague through you. N
I will tell you what I will do: I will cut off your h
with my sword. If this succeeds, then are you no G
and you can go free; but if you terrify me so I can
do it, then is it plain you are a God, and guilty of
charge.' But Apollonius heeded none of these thir
and conversed with Damis about the delta of the N
Ælianus sent for him again immediately, and had l
placed in the 'free prison' where the inmates were p
mitted all the freedom consistent with safety.

　　When Apollonius entered it, he immediately sym
thized with the sorrows of the discouraged men aro
him, and after having patiently listened to the stories
several he addressed them all from time to time, exh
ing them firstly to dismiss fear which only increased t'
sufferings, being itself a sort of slow death; second,
horting them to patience and endurance, an invention
the Gods themselves. Then he reminded them that, a
all, life itself was a sort of prison out of which it
well to be delivered, and that most of the noble
great men of all times had at some time or another b
imprisoned and ill-used, so that they surely could aff
to endure the present sufferings. This speech so rai
their spirits that many dried their tears, and felt relie
of their troubles while Apollonius stayed near them.

The Emperor sent into the prison a spy who feigned
...e accused of heavy crimes. But Apollonius discerned
...plot, and said nothing that could have furthered the
...poses of the spy, speaking mainly of forests, mount-
...s and flowers. And when the spy directly sought to
...1 him to utter imprecations against the Emperor, A-
...lonius said, 'Friend, say what thou desirest; I will
...betray thee. As for me, I will tell the Emperor my-
...' what I may have to tell him.'

About the fifth day that he was in prison a man came
...retly from Ælianus to him, once more warning Apo-
...ius not to manifest any scorn of the Emperor when
...should meet him, and to be prepared for harshness or
...ghness of voice. Thanking for the good advice Apo-
...ius retired early.

By dawn came a messenger from the Emperor warn-
...him to be ready to face the Emperor about noon. A-
...lonius rested again, saying to Damis he had had a bad
...ht trying to remember something Phraotes had once
...1 him. 'You had better be thinking about your defen-
...so as not to have to speak entirely *ex tempore*,' anxi-
...ly said Damis. But Apollonius retorted, 'Why should
...ot speak *ex tempore?* Do I know that of which he
...1 accuse me? I was trying to remember something
...ich, after all, suits this occasion very well: that the

tamers of lions must neither beat them, nor coax them;
but treat them firmly gently.' 'Ah yes,' said Damis 'but
I remember another lion, in the fable of Æsop, who
feigned himself sick; but .the fox noticed that all the
tracks led into the cave, but none out of it.' 'But the
fox would have been more cunning still had he entered
the cave, and managed to leave it safely, and warned o-
thers.'

Apollonius was permitted to go to the palace unbound
with four soldiers and Damis following at some distance.
While waiting in the palace Apollonius was self-possess-
ed and observant. 'The whole palace strikes me as a
bath: those who are outside want to go in, as if they
were unwashed; those who are within seek to leave it, as
if they had been washed out.' As Damis seemed to be
very cast down Apollonius said to him, 'You seem to
have little genius for dying, apparently, although you
have philosophized by my side ever since our youth.   I
supposed you would have known all my tactics by this
time. And as soldiers need not only courage, but tactics
also, so does a philosopher need not only courage and
philosophy, but discernment also, to tell what his right
time of dying is—so that he neither seek it, nor flee it.
And you know well that for dying I have chosen a time
consistent with best philosophy.'

When Apollonius was ushered into the Emperor's presence the latter was just sacrificing to Athene in the 'court of Adonis'; looking backwards he was surprised at sight of the strange figure. He cried out, 'Ælianus, you have introduced here a God.' Apollonius spoke forth: 'Then Athene has not yet lifted from your eyes the mists that you might discern Gods from men.' 'And,' retorted Domitian, 'how is it with you, that you consider my worst enemies your Gods?' And what enmity could there ever be between you and Phraotes and Iarchas whom alone I consider worthy of the name of Gods?' 'Digress not to the sages of India, but speak to me of Nerva, and of the companions of his guilt.' 'If you desire to discover what I know of the matter, listen; for why should I hide the truth from you?' And Domitian thought he was about to hear weighty matters.

'I know Nerva to be a most moderate man, most devoted to you, avoiding wealth and high positions as sources of danger. And his friends, for I suppose you talk of Rufus and Orphitus, are said to be likewise.' At this Domitian flew into a rage, asserted he had knowledge so exact about their plots and sacrifices that he knew as much as if he had been present. He himself, however, was no sycophant, and the truth would be found out at the public hearing.

Calmly Apollonius answered that it was shameful for the Emperor to hold a hearing if he was convinced of what he thought he knew; and if he was about to hold a hearing to find the truth, why should he consider himself convinced in advance? Also that he desired to defend himself against the Emperor's accusations.

Domitian replied, 'Begin thy defence from anywhere thou pleasest; I also know where I shall end up at, and what I must now begin with.' He commanded the guards to maltreat Apollonius. They cut off his beard and hair, and bound him as tightly as any criminal. As his hair was being cut, he exclaimed, 'I did not know I was risking my life on account of my hair.' While being bound he said, 'If I be a magician, why dost thou have me bound? Could such bonds hold me?' But Domitian said, 'Thou shalt not be untied until thou have become water, or a rock, or a tree.' Apollonius retorted, 'Even if I could do this I would not do it until I had conducted the defense of these innocent men whom thou accusest falsely.' 'But who will conduct thy own defense?' And Apollonius answered with sublime calmness, 'Time, and the Will of the Gods, and the Love of the Wisdom to which I am united.'

Apollonius was sent back to prison, and after several days a Syracusan spy came in, with the same purpose as

the former one, but dealing more directly, sympathysing
with Apollonius' misfortunes, and his having been falsely
accused to the Emperor. But Apollonius said he was
more grieved at once having been accused falsely by Euphrates to the Gymnosophits, so that he almost missed
seeing them. 'What,' said the spy, 'are you more griev-'
ed at having been falsely accused to the Gymnosophists,
than to the Emperor?' 'Yes,' said Apollonius, 'for there
I went to learn, while here I came to teach.'. And what
are you to teach here? 'That I am an honest man; for if.
I have been chained for being an honest man, how much
more would I not have been chained if I had told un-
truths?'

Damis was heart-broken, seeing no salvation. 'O Tyanian, what will happen to us?' 'Just the same that has
happened to us—we shall not be killed.' 'And who is
sufficiently unwoundable? When will you be set free?'
'According to the Judge, to-day; according to me, right
now.'. And Apollonius slipped his foot out of the chain,
just to assure Damis he was really free, and then slipped
his foot back into the chain. 'This is a proof of my freedom; take courage.'

The same day came a messenger announcing that at
the advice of Ælianus the Emperor permitted Apollonius
to be freed from the chains and to be re-placed in the

'free prison.' He was received by its inmates as a father
might have been received by his children, with tears and
embraces. Nor did he cease giving them good advice.

. The next day he told Damis that he expected to be
set free after the trial, which was to take place in four
days. He instructed Damis to go to Dikaearchia by land
and there await him. 'Dead or alive?' anxiously inquired
Damis. 'Resurrected, as you may think; but as I think
alive.' Much against his will did Damis obey, neither
despairing entirely, nor hoping much. On arriving at his
destination he found that a terrific storm had been raging
on the sea, so that he must have perished had he gone
that way.

During these four days a beautiful episode occured in
the prison. A Messenian youth of exceptional beauty
had by his father been sent to Rome to learn Roman ju-
risprudence. Domitian had seen him, and fallen in love
with him;but the youth was modest, guarded his strength
and refused all gifts. Many others fell in love with him
not hesitating thus to become rivals of the Emperor who
finding the youth obdurate shut him up in prison. He
addressed Apollonius, and soon a helpful conversation
was in progress.The sage,seeing how modestly the youth
behaved and conversed, and how he blushed in recounting the facts of his misfortune, did not ask him such que-

stions about his opinion of love between men, but ₋ asked him if he did not own many slaves in Arcadia? 'Many.' What do you think you are to them? 'The laws make me their master.' Must not slaves obey the masters of their body? The youth answered, 'I know that the power of tyrants is hard; and therefore also do they extend their power over free men. But I am the master of my body, and propose to keep it undefiled.' But how wilt thou accomplish this, seeing thou hast a lover who woos thy youth with a sword? 'I will offer it my neck, which is made for a sword.' Then Apollonius praised him, 'I recognize in thee a true Arcadian.'— The upshot of the youth's difficulties was that he was released, and returned home with honour; where, on account of his beauty, he became more famous than those youths who in Lacedaemon voluntarily offer their naked backs to the whip as a trial of endurance.

EIGHTH BOOK

The Assumption

On the morning of the trial Apollonius was in hi
place in the court-room prepared to hold a conversatio
rather than for a fight for life or death. For on the roa
he had asked the scribe 'Whither are we going?' To th
court-room. 'Against whom shall I have to defend my
self?' Against thy accusers, and the Emperor will decide
'But who will decide between the Emperor and me? fo
I will show that he has wronged philosophy.'

- As he entered the court-room another scribe came u
and commanded him to enter naked. 'Are we going t
the bath, or to the court-room?' Nay, said the scribe
not without clothes, but without magic amulets, or th
like.

The court-room was crowded with the best people o
Rome, because the Emperor desired that Apolloni
should be convicted as publicly as possible in order
justify his intended measures against Nerva. Apolloni
himself paid so little attention to the people or to th
Emperor that he did not even look at them. The accu
er, a freed-man of Euphrates', noticing this, commande

him to look at the 'God of all men.' But Apollonius looked at the ceiling, implying that he was already looking up to Zeus, and that tne Emperor was worse than the flatterers, in that he permitted himself to be thus flattered.

Domitian passed over most of the points of the accusation, as beneath his notice. But he asked Apollonius why he clothed himself differently from other men, in linen, not in wool? 'Because I do not desire to be a burdeh to animals, but permit the earth to nourish and clothe me.' Second, Why do people call you a God? 'Because any man is considered good is called by that name.' Third, about the plague at Ephesus; from what reasons, and in what manner, did you predict it? 'Because I live simply and eat little did I the first perceive its approach. Do you desire I should tell you the causes of the plague?' But Domitian, fearful lest Apollonius should attribute it to some of his crimes, said he did not care to know. He then came to the fourth question, about the alleged night sacrifice of a boy. He delayed a good deal, and then asked it indirectly, as it were to catch Apollonius unawares. But he spoke out courageously, as if scolding a school-boy, showing the self-contradiction of the accusation; and he spoke so sincerely that he was rewarded by acclamations of the people far louder than were custom-

ary in the imperial court-room. Domitian was cowed ᴉ
this, and hastily said, 'I absolve thee; yet stay here th
I may question thee further.' But Apollonius declar￼
that this was hardly just, and, demanding freedom, d￼
appeared out of the court-room.

Having thus left the court-room at noon, he appear￼
to Demetrius and Damis in Dikaearchia. Damis had aꜞ
ived the day before, and had communicated all he kne
to Demetrius, and though they both had confidence
anything Apollonius might say, yet was it with but sm
hope that they followed his instructions in going to t
sea-shore. But even wile Damis was saying 'O Go
shall we ever again see the splendidly honourable frienc
Apollonius stood right near him, and said, 'Ye see hi
already.' 'Art thou alive?' asked Demetrius, 'if thou
dead we have not yet ceased mourning for thee.' Th
Apollonius reached out his hand to show he was no ᴀ
parition, and they fell on his neck, and kissed him. ᴉ
declared he had defended himself and conquered; tⵑ
this defense had taken place only a few hours ago, as t
day had advanced to only shortly after noon. 'But hoᵂ
asked Demetrius, have you travelled over so great a dꞔ
tance in so short time?' Apollonius ascribed this to t
Divinity, and recounted everything in order on the w
home. Demetrius, on his side, recounted a dream whꜞ

Telesinus had had in which Apollonius alone of all the philosophers had escaped a river of fire by swimming through it.

Demetrius feared that this escape of Apollonius' was only a temporary one, and that Domitian would have him pursued; but Apollonius assured him of the contrary remarking that such natures as the Emperor's, being unaccustomed to anything but flattery were cowed by hearing the truth at times. But he requested that he might have a bed to lie down upon inasmuch as, said he, he had not bent the knee since his battle. So on arriving at home, after encouraging the others to eat, and after making his prayers to Apollo, he slept as peacefully as a child.

In the morning Apollonius declared that it was his purpose to take ship for Greece; but Demetrius thought it too dangerous a journey, as being too public. But the unterrifiable Apollonius insisted that if the whole earth really did belong to the tyrant it was better to die in the light than to live in obscurity. So, with much regret saying farewell, having past Syracuse and Messenia, they came to the mouths of the river Alpheus, and went to Olympia to the temple of Zeus. Here many came to see him from all parts of Greece. The most contradictory rumors had spread abroad about his fate and thousands flocked to see him again. But what made most people almost reverence him as a God was the quiet way in which he spoke about his experiences in Rome, without the least boastfulness.

Among those who came to see him was a youth who asked him if Zeus was favourable to the Emperor? He answered it was better not to talk of such things in the sanctuary. Another inquired if the Gods approved of the Athenians for having declared certain men by name of Harmodius and Aristogiton for 'fathers of their fatherland.' The answer was that he thought as little of them as if by free vote of the majority of the people the common tyrant had been elected in their place.

It happened that their common funds were running low, and Damis warned Apollonius of this state of affairs. The latter, with permission of the priests, took from the sanctuary one thousand drachmas. They declared that the Divinity was angry not because he had taken so much, but because he had taken so little.

Having spent fourty days in conversation and good deeds in the temple, he decided to go to Lebadaea, to the temple of Trophimus, where he had never before been. The priests of this temple, however, refused to initiate him on the grounds of his being a magician. But he went by night to the opening of that cave, bent back

ar of the iron bars and, clad in his philosopher's man-
e, he entered the cave alone. He remained there quite
little time, and when he came out he held in his arms
book. In entering the cave his question had been What
the most beautiful Virtue, and the purest Philosophy?
e returned with pages covered with writings which set
rth the Pythagorean manner of life, so that even divine
thority recommended his system of philosophy. This
ook is still preserved in Antium, as a great rarity, deser-
ng the greatest reverence. Others suppose that the em-
ror Hadrian had taken this book with many other va-
able written relics of Apollonius to his favourite palace
Actium.

Little by little all his former disciples gathered around
m out of all Ionia, forming a sect of Apollonians, as
ey came to be called. Even Rhetoric stood with them
ill-repute, and they confined themselves to publicly
king their Master questions which he never failed to
swer wisely and well.

When some made it an accusation against him that he
ade it his practice to go into the desert out of the way
officials and the military governors, he answered that
did so in order that the wolves and bears should not
ll upon the flock. For during his Roman imprisonment
e had become convinced that the public men of his day

became rich so easily, and so played upon the hopes and
fears of the people that he preferred that his 'disciples
should have nothing to do with them.

About this time, while he was still active in Hellas, a
prodigy occurred in the sky: a crown, like a sun-born
rainbow surrounded the disk of the sun, darkening its
rays. It was by the people generally accepted as a divine warning of changes in the rulership of the Empire.
The Governor of Hellas, having learnt to appreciate A-
pollonius, begged him to reveal its significance; but all
that he would say was, 'Fear not; light will come out of
this darkness.'

After a two year's stay in Hellas Apollonius went to
Ionia, staying most of the time in Ephesus and Smyrna,
going wherever he was really wanted, blessing, and being blessed.

The manner of Domitian's death was seen by Apollonius in Ephesus, and he announced it to the crowd to
whom he happened to be preaching. They were at first
incredulous, but when confirmation arrived worshipped
him all the more.

A month later, when Nerva was safe on the imperial
throne he invited Apollonius to help him rule, but Apollonius kindly but firmly refused, with a rather obscure
saying. And indeed Nerva ruled only one year and four

months. Yet not to have the appearance of neglecting a true friend and worthy ruler he wrote him a long letter full of the worthiest advice.

Then he called Damis and made him the messenger. Damis obeyed, but it went against his better self; for he had a sort of premonition that he would not see his beloved Master again. But there was nothing for him to do but to obey, and evidently Apollonius was preparing to retire into complete obscurity, according to his own precept, *Seek to live obscurely*. In order to pass away out of life without witnesses he therefore sent Damis away, saying these significant words, 'O Damis, when thou shalt philosophize for thyself keep me before thine eyes.'

Although Apollonius was by some said to have reached the age of from eighty to one hundred years yet were not his powers weakened, nor his mind dulled. True, the statue in the temple at Tyana shows many wrinkles on his forehead but his age was said to have been more prolific than the youth of the brilliant Alcibiades.

According to some he died at Ephesus, served by two female slaves. Others again say he passed away in Lindus, where he had gone into the temple of Athene, and disappeared in it. Others, however, insist that he passed away in Crete, in a manner still more wonderful than that in Lindus. It was reported that he came to the tem-

ple of the Diktynna by night-time, which was watched
over by dogs more fierce than bears. Yet they did not
bark at him, but came up and fawned on him—wherea
the temple-authorities bound him, for being a magician
and thief, in that he had thus influenced the dogs. Bu
he freed himself and called to himself the men and priest
who had bound him, so that nothing should be done in
corner. Then the doors of the temple opened themselve
to him without the help of human hands; and when he
had hurried within, they closed on him; and from within
the marvelling priests heard the voices of maidens sing
ing *Ascend into heaven from earth, ascend!*

Yea, even after he had, according to the manner of
mortals, passed away, did he yet philosophize about the
soul and immortality. There was a youth in Tyana who
was powerful in debate, but did not agree to the tru
doctrine of the soul and immortality. After quite extend
ed reasonings about the subject among the Tyanian youth
he declared it could not be so inasmuch as Apolloniu
was so thoroughly dead that he could not appear to any
body, although for ten months he himself had besough
Apollonius to appear to him, if the immortality of the
soul was a true doctrine. Five days later, having once
more discussed the matter, he fell asleep while discussing
and was awakened with so great a start that perspiratio

rolled from his face, crying out, 'Do you not see Apollonius, how he is watching your studies, and singing marvellous rhapsodies about the soul?' But the others could not see Apollonius; but the youth gave them what he caught of Apollonius' song:

Not to thee, but to Providence, belongs the soul.

After the body has fallen, like to the swiftest horses

Free from her bonds, she hastens away, and mixes herself to the fluid air repelling for ever

The worn-out and pressing yoke of patient servitude.

Yet of what use is to you what you shall see when you are no more?

Or to what end this searching and seeking while still you are among the living?

A grave of Apollonius is not to be found anywhere, although indeed there are marvellous legends about him everywhere. Also there is a temple in his honour at Tyana, erected by the Emperors who thought him not unworthy to be honoured in a manner in which they themselves were later honoured.

CPSIA information can be obtained
at www.ICGtesting.com
Printed in the USA
LVHW020902260121
677443LV00018B/3404